TRADITIONAL STORIES OF THE ARCTIC AND SUBARCTIC NATIONS

BY MARIE POWELL

CONTENT CONSULTANT
Ronald Brower Sr.
Iñupiaq Language Instructor
University of Alaska Fairbanks

Core Library

An Imprint of Abdo Publishing
abdopublishing.com

Cover image: Two Inuit throat singers pose wearing traditional clothing.

abdopublishing.com

Published by Abdo Publishing, a division of ABDO, PO Box 398166, Minneapolis, Minnesota 55439. Copyright © 2018 by Abdo Consulting Group, Inc. International copyrights reserved in all countries. No part of this book may be reproduced in any form without written permission from the publisher. Core Library™ is a trademark and logo of Abdo Publishing.

Printed in the United States of America, North Mankato, Minnesota
052017
092017

THIS BOOK CONTAINS
RECYCLED MATERIALS

Cover Photo: Marilyn Angel WynnNativeStock
Interior Photos: Marilyn Angel WynnNativeStock, 1; North Wind Picture Archives, 4–5; M. Cornelius/Shutterstock Images, 7; iStockphoto, 8–9, 29, 43; Red Line Editorial, 12–13, 33; Sepp Friedhuber/iStockphoto, 14–15; Hinrich Baesemann/picture-alliance/dpa/AP Images, 18; Paul Nicklen/National Geographic/Getty Images, 20–21; Carlo Allegri/Canadian Press/AP Images, 24; Paul Watson/Toronto Star/Getty Images, 26–27, 31, 45; Patrick Endres/Alaska Stock/Design Pics Inc/Alamy, 36–37; Gilles Mingasson/Getty Images News/Getty Images, 39; Sophia Granchinho/Shutterstock Images, 40

Editor: Arnold Ringstad
Imprint Designer: Maggie Villaume
Series Design Direction: Ryan Gale

Publisher's Cataloging-in-Publication Data

Names: Powell, Marie, author.
Title: Traditional stories of the Arctic and Subarctic nations / by Marie Powell.
Description: Minneapolis, MN : Abdo Publishing, 2018. | Series: Native American oral histories | Includes bibliographical references and index.
Identifiers: LCCN 2017930244 | ISBN 9781532111709 (lib. bdg.) | ISBN 9781680789553 (ebook)
Subjects: LCSH: Indians of North America--Juvenile literature. | Indians of North America--Social life and customs--Juvenile literature. | Indian mythology--North America--Juvenile literature. | Indians of North America--Folklore--Juvenile literature.
Classification: DDC 979--dc23
LC record available at http://lccn.loc.gov/2017930244

CONTENTS

STORIES AS MEMORY

The northern lights glow above the winter landscape. The polar ice holds many stories. So do the people who have survived on this land for centuries. The storyteller's voice rises and falls. These words have been spoken over and over again.

The storyteller may recount a memory from his or her life. A hunter may tell the story of a whale hunt. Or a tale might feature strange creatures, powerful beings, or people with great strength or abilities. The stories of the Arctic and Subarctic Nations carry with them the traditions and beliefs of these cultures.

A sketch from a European artist shows how an Inuit storyteller performed in the 1800s.

TRUE NORTHERNERS

The far north of North America can be both harsh and beautiful. It has two regions, the Arctic and the Subarctic. The Arctic stretches across 5.5 million square miles (14.5 million sq km). It includes the North Pole and parts of three oceans. Earth's tilt means that in some areas, the sun sets for weeks at a time in winter. In the summer, it may remain in the sky for just as long. The Subarctic region lies south of the Arctic Circle. It includes Alaska and

NORTHERN LIGHTS

The northern lights, or the aurora borealis, appear in the sky throughout the Arctic and Subarctic regions. These bands of colored light occur near Earth's magnetic poles. They happen when particles from the sun collide with Earth's atmosphere. There are many stories about the northern lights. The Inuit call them *arsaniit*, or the spirits of animals they've hunted. They tell stories about sky people playing ball games. In the Iñupiaq language, they are sometimes known as *kiguyait*. Cree and Iñupiat beliefs say the lights are the dancing spirits of the dead.

In the far north, the sun sometimes hangs in the sky for weeks at a time.

northern Canada. This landscape features tundra and evergreen forests.

Some 20 Native Nations live in the Arctic and Subarctic. Major Arctic Nations include the Inuit, Iñupiat, Yupik, and Unangan (Aleut). Major Subarctic Nations

The northern lights appear in the sky over Yellowknife, Canada.

include the Innu, Gwich'in, Dene, Woodland Cree (Sakawithiniwak), and Ojibwa (Anishinaabe). Historically, people would come together to live in villages in winter. In summer, many people traveled around, living a nomadic lifestyle.

CULTURAL TIES

The stories of these nations have many meanings. They are often short and dramatic. A story may tell about creation, animals, hunting, love, death, or the afterlife. Stories often hold a deeper message about how to

A HUNTER'S SHOE

Three scraps of hide lay hidden in rocks on an ice field near Aishihik Lake, Yukon. In 2003, researchers found, cleaned, and tested this material. They suspect it came from a caribou. They tried to re-create its shape. They soon realized it was part of a moccasin, a type of shoe. It was approximately 1,400 years old. This made it the oldest moccasin in Canada. The researchers also found arrows and throwing darts nearby. This told them the area was likely a summer hunting ground. The moccasin is one of many artifacts that tell stories about the region's past.

behave or about family life. Members of these nations who know the region and languages may understand the meanings best. Men or women, old or young, may tell stories.

Storytellers may use the rhythms of the person who first told them the story. They use gestures to act out the story. They may even make the sounds of wind or wildlife. Today, traditional Arctic and Subarctic stories are told in person, in film and television, and in books. The stories help preserve and share people's cultures.

STRAIGHT TO THE
SOURCE

Herman Michell is a Woodlands Cree author who can still recall his mother telling stories in the same way her relatives, teachers, and elders told them:

> *Winter is a time when certain stories are told in northern Bush Cree trapping families. My thoughts travel back in time. I remember shadows of movement on cabin walls, the smell of wood smoke, and the sounds from fire humming the night into being. The stories would begin. Slowly at first, quietly, picking up momentum at times, thought-provoking words unleashed, followed by inaudible whispers, deep sighs, leaving footprints in minds to interpret. Time blurs in unknown story spaces. Words illuminate a colorful tapestry of people, places, and experiences unfolding into the present. Storytelling is a way of passing on knowledge.*

> Source: Herman Michell. "Bush Cree Storytelling Methodology." *In Education* 21.2 (2015). Web. Accessed January 19, 2017.

Point of View
How does the writer describe the experience of hearing stories as a child? Why does he say stories are important? Read back through the chapter. Do you agree? Why or why not?

ARCTIC AND SUBARCTIC NATIONS

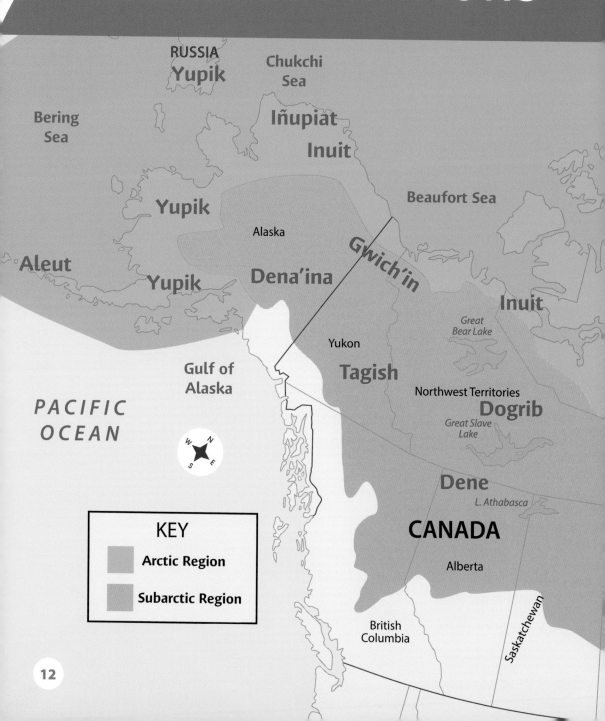

RUSSIA

Yupik

Chukchi Sea

Bering Sea

Iñupiat

Inuit

Yupik

Beaufort Sea

Alaska

Gwich'in

Aleut

Yupik

Dena'ina

Inuit

Great Bear Lake

Yukon

Tagish

Gulf of Alaska

Northwest Territories

Dogrib

Great Slave Lake

PACIFIC OCEAN

W N E S

Dene

L. Athabasca

CANADA

Alberta

KEY

Arctic Region

Subarctic Region

British Columbia

Saskatchewan

Inuit

GREENLAND
(Denmark)

Inuit

Baffin
Bay

Inuit

Inuit

Nunavut

Inuit

Inuit

Inuit

Labrador
Sea

Inuit

Inuit

Hudson
Bay

Innu

Manitoba

Newfoundland

Cree

Innu

Cree

Quebec

Ontario

Ojibwa

Cree

CHAPTER
TWO

STORIES FROM THE SEA

Many people in the Arctic and Subarctic regions are dependent on the sea. The animals that live in or near the sea have long been important to people's survival. Legendary water creatures commonly appear in these cultures' stories.

SEA MOTHER

Inuit stories tells of Sedna, the Sea Mother. In Iñupiat traditions, she is also known as Siraggina, or Uiluaqtaq. There are many versions of tales about her. One tells how Sedna became a sea spirit. In this story, a married woman's father visits her. He finds her

Icy coastlines and real-world animals likely inspired many traditional stories.

so unhappy that he decides to take her back home. But the woman's husband changes himself into a seabird and follows them. He causes a storm and she falls overboard. She sinks to the bottom and becomes a sea spirit. Her fingers become sea animals.

Sedna is described as having long, tangled hair. This feature appears in some Inuit beliefs. When hunters cannot catch seals or fish, it is thought that Sedna is upset with the people. Then a shaman will make contact with Sedna. The shaman will comb her hair so she will be happy again.

PERSPECTIVES

BIRD HELPERS: LOONS

Inuit stories tell of boys who are blind regaining sight with the help of loons. For example, Lumaaq is a boy who is blind and abused by his family. He shoots a polar bear, but his mother tells him he shot the dog. She gives him only a small amount of meat. But he knows it is from a polar bear. Then she leaves him alone and starving. Loons find him. In one version of the story, they dive into the sea with him several times. On the third dive, he can see again.

FIRST AND LAST PERSON

The Inuit tell many stories about Kiviuq, a hero and a shaman. He is known as the first and last person on Earth. In one story, a young orphan boy is bullied until his grandmother teaches him to pretend to be a seal. He lures people out to sea to hunt him, then the grandmother causes a storm. Kiviuq is the only one who survives. In some versions of the story, Kiviuq is the only one

WINTER OR SUMMER

In the far north, the sea is important in both winter and summer. The Arctic char, seals, whales, walrus, polar bears, and other sea animals are important to the Inuit. Seals provide skins for boots or tents. They also give oil for fuel and meat for food. In winter, below-freezing temperatures cause fish-eating birds and animals to migrate. One of them, the Arctic tern, has the farthest migration of any animal. Some caribou travel in search of lichen to eat. Animals that remain all winter include ravens, Arctic foxes, Arctic wolves, musk oxen, lemmings, polar bears, and ringed seals.

Kayaking remains an important part of life in many coastal Arctic and Subarctic Nations.

who didn't bully the boy. In other versions he is the

seal boy himself. He finds himself paddling his kayak

alone on the ocean with no land in sight. Then he sees

a sandpiper, a bird that is one of his helping spirits. He follows the sandpiper. At first he sees only dark water. But he keeps following the sandpiper. Eventually he finds land.

Kiviuq has many adventures. He is known as an immortal hero. The stories are partly about creation. Some show how sea ice and fog were first created. They also demonstrate parts of Inuit culture. Stories feature kayaks used to navigate dangerous waters. Kiviuq stories contain important advice, too. Some tell how to hunt seals at their breathing holes in the ice.

EXPLORE ONLINE

This chapter discussed the Arctic and Subarctic Nations' relationship with the sea. The website below includes more information about these Nations' lives. It also has images of artifacts and objects that the Nations used in their daily lives in the past. What new information can you learn from this website?

NATIONAL MUSEUM OF THE AMERICAN INDIAN: INFINITY OF NATIONS

abdocorelibrary.com/arctic-and-subarctic-nations

STRANGE CREATURES

Stories about creatures and people with extraordinary abilities are popular in all cultures. Many of the creatures in the Arctic and Subarctic Nations' stories relate to local environments. For example, the Inuit depend on the sea for hunting. They have many names for sea ice. *Siku* is loose sea ice, and *tuvaq* is landlocked ice. The Inuit also know of the sea's dangers. Stories about sea creatures warn children against playing near it.

GIANTS ON LAND AND SEA

Many Inuit stories have giant dogs, birds, or people in them. For instance, large seabirds might steal people's clothing or belongings

Inuit hunters pull a narwhal from the sea.

MAN'S BEST FRIEND

Dogs and dog sleds are important in the North. Dogs are still used, but today many hunters rely on snowmobiles and all-terrain vehicles. Some hunters believe the dog teams were better because they also helped the hunters. Dogs used their keen sense of smell and natural abilities to help hunters find prey. The dogs' senses and instincts also helped them find their way in dangerous conditions.

or even carry people away. In one story, a giant gull carries a hunter away. After the hunter kills it, he isn't afraid of anything. In other stories, male and female giants have adventures with hunters. Their size often helps them capture animals or save the day. A giantess hunts whales and bears. She places her human husband in her boot to keep him safe. Some who study these stories also connect modern legends of mysterious creatures with Inuit stories of the Tuniit. These were the people said to have inhabited the land before the Inuit. They are described as thick, strong, and dressed in skins.

LEGENDARY HUMANS AND ANIMALS

Many Inuit stories show how people should live or relate to one another. The legend of Qallupilluit tells of a woman who lives in the sea. She has green skin and long fingernails. She wears an *amauti*, a parka with a special pouch near the hood to carry children. If children go too near the shore, she will capture them. She puts them in her parka and takes them into the sea.

In one version of the story, a grandmother grows

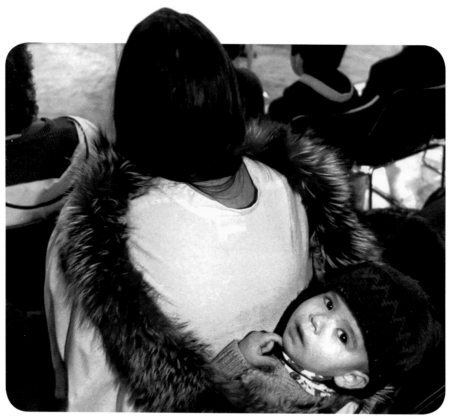

An infant sits in its mother's amauti.

angry with her grandson. She calls Qallupilluit to take him away. Later she wants him back and asks hunters to help her. They watch for him to appear in the cracks of ice. They try several times to sneak up on him and finally cut the seaweed that holds him to Qallupilluit. The grandson grows up to become a great hunter.

Legendary characters also appear in the stories of the Iñupiat people. Qulipiluk is a sea troll. Tiritchiq is a dragon-like creature. Qalutchaq is a mermaid who also appears in Inuit tales.

The Cree Subarctic culture shares stories of Wîshâkechâk. Wîshâkechâk is a trickster, a mythological being that can transform into people or animals such as the raven, coyote, or rabbit. He also has other powers, such as creating the world from mud brought up from the bottom of floodwaters. The Wendigo of the Cree and Ojibwa peoples is a spirit or supernatural monster that eats people.

FURTHER EVIDENCE

This chapter talks about the importance of the sea to the Inuit people. What was one of the main points of the chapter? Take a look at the map on this website. Find the information about sea ice, and read or listen to the words spoken directly by the people of the area. How do you think some of these stories about creatures came about? Find a quote on this website that helps you understand the stories.

SEA ICE ATLAS
abdocorelibrary.com/arctic-and-subarctic-nations

STORIES AS KNOWLEDGE

Their traditional ways of life, along with the stories that came from these traditions, have helped the Nations of the Arctic and Subarctic survive through changing times. Stories helped pass along details of family life, survival skills, and culture. They also helped record details of these regions' landscapes.

SHARING CULTURE

There are many Nations within the Arctic and Subarctic. One Canadian territory, the Yukon, has 14 communities with 8 different languages. Each Nation has some variations

Stories and other traditions help pass along culture to a younger generation.

THROAT SINGING

Two women face each other. One woman begins breathing in and out in a short rhythm. The other follows. This practice is called throat singing. Inuit women use it to sing babies to sleep or as a winter contest or game. They might use words or syllables, wildlife sounds, or sounds from daily living. This cultural tradition had been banned by local Christian priests in the early 1900s. It has been revived since the 1980s.

on shared stories along with completely different stories.

In one Tagish story, Game Mother lived with her husband and brothers. They made her snowshoes, but she didn't want to travel. Every night she put them under her pillow. In the morning the snowshoes were unraveled again. Finally her family made her a camp. When the men left, animals began to appear. The moose had grizzly bear teeth, so Game Mother took out its teeth and showed it how to eat willow. Then came the caribou, the sheep, the grizzly bear, the wolf, and the rabbit. She showed them all how to eat and behave. Then she made them a big

Moose live throughout the Subarctic region.

swing or hammock. She hung it from four mountains. They sang and danced together and then went to find their homes. This story shows the connections between people and animals. These connections are still important to the Arctic and Subarctic Nations.

Many names of places have a story connected to them. Storytellers link their family histories with the places where they have traveled. Clans feel they own certain stories, and clan members retell these stories with details of place and time. Some storytellers say they follow traditional stories "like a map" in order to tell them exactly as their elders did.

SURVIVING CONTACT

Early contact with Europeans caused problems for the Nations of the Arctic and Subarctic. For example, in 1741 the Russians claimed southwest Alaska. They forced the Unangan to relocate. The Unangan depended on fishing and seal hunting. Artifacts have shown they had lived in the area for more than 3,000 years. Russia sold this area to the United States in 1867.

In Canada and in the United States, residential schools had an impact on most Nations. For approximately 100 years, Arctic and Subarctic children were taken from their homes. They were forced to live

Inuit artist Susie Malgokak creates images to preserve her memories from life before she was forced to attend a residential school.

in schools far from their families. Bob Baxter of Thunder Bay, Ontario, belongs to the Anishinaabe group of tribes. He recalls the way stories were woven into their lives before he was taken to residential school: "When I think back to my childhood, it brings back memories. . . . And the things that I remember, [are] the legends at night that my dad used to tell us, stories."

At the residential schools, children were not allowed to wear traditional clothes, speak their languages, or take part in ceremonies. Many were abused. In 2005 they sued the Canadian government. The stories of survivors became the evidence that helped bring justice. In 2007 the government set up a fund for the 80,000 survivors. On June 11, 2008, Canadian prime minister Stephen Harper formally apologized to those who had been mistreated.

CHANGES

Changes in the northern ecosystem are having an effect on the Inuit way of life and storytelling. Climate change

NUNAVUT

Nunavut is Canada's northernmost territory. Inuit people and other members of Native Nations make up most of its approximately 37,000 people. The region covers more than 808,000 square miles (2.1 million sq km). The capital is Iqaluit. What does the map suggest about the way of life for people who live in this area? How might modern developments have changed daily life here?

- Alert
- Ellesmere Island
- GREENLAND
- ARCTIC OCEAN
- Grise Fiord
- Baffin Bay
- Devon I.
- Melville I.
- Resolute
- Lancaster Sound
- Arctic Bay
- Nanisivik
- Pond Inlet
- Clyde River
- Davis Strait
- Viscount Melville Sound
- Somerset Island
- Qikiqtarjuaq
- Baffin Island
- Prince of Wales I.
- Gulf of Boothia
- McClintock Channel
- Pangnirtung
- Victoria Island
- King William I.
- Igloolik
- Cambridge Bay
- Taloyoak
- Hall Beach
- Gjoa Haven
- Kugaaruk
- Foxe Basin
- IQALUIT
- Coronation Gulf
- Queen Maud Gulf
- Umingmaktok
- Repulse Bay
- Cape Dorset
- Bathurst Inlet
- Hudson Strait
- Coral Harbour
- Southampton Island
- Baker Lake
- NORTHWEST TERRITORIES
- Dubawnt Lake
- Chesterfield Inlet
- Rankin Inlet
- Whale Cove
- Hudson Bay
- Arviat

is melting the sea ice. It is causing physical changes to the land. This process results from the release of greenhouse gases into the atmosphere by vehicles and industries.

These gases trap heat in the atmosphere. This gradually warms the climate.

The Native Nations of the north face other challenges too. A record increase in the population of Inuit in Nunavut caused housing shortages starting in the 2010s. But storytelling traditions remain strong. Native storytelling and culture are becoming part of school studies and festivals across the North.

CARIBOU

Caribou, or reindeer, have lived in North America for 1.8 million years. They can be found in most Canadian provinces, especially in the tundra and boreal forest areas. Both males and females have antlers. Some caribou stay in one spot year-round. Others migrate to give birth to calves. In the last 20 years, large numbers of caribou have disappeared. The loss has been caused by changes in the weather and environment, increased predators, and human development. Scientists are working to save the caribou.

STRAIGHT TO THE
SOURCE

Inuit author Michael Kusugak shares stories because he feels they are important:

My writing and storytelling has always been driven by the stories told to me by my grandmother when I was a boy. When I was small we still lived a traditional life living in igloo, sod huts and skin tents. We traveled by dog team searching for game to keep us fed and clothed. At night my grandmother would tell me stories to put me to sleep.

These stories are being lost now. We no longer travel by dog team or live in igloos. We live in houses now, with heat and electricity. We also have new storytellers, storytellers from the south that enter our homes through the TV and Internet. Our children are modern children in an ancient land.

Source: Michael Arvaarluk Kusugak. "Teacher's Guide." *Vancouver International Children's Festival. VICF, 2015. Web. Accessed January 20, 2017.*

Back It Up
The author of this passage is using evidence to support a point. Write a paragraph describing the point the author is making. Then write down two or three pieces of evidence the author uses to make the point.

STORIES TODAY

Stories influence the lives of northern Native Nations peoples today. Festivals and storytelling events are held throughout the Arctic and Subarctic regions. People wear traditional clothing. They perform songs and dances. Storytellers present tales both old and new to their audiences.

CLIMATE CHANGE

The Inuit are deeply familiar with the climate of northern North America. Researchers and scientists consult with the Inuit and other Arctic and Subarctic peoples about it. An Inuit person might know if a storm is coming by the way

A traditional blanket tossing event is held at the end of Iñupiat whaling festivals.

clouds scatter, for instance. Climate changes today are also altering the patterns the Inuit know. Local people are working with Native and non-Native scientists to study what patterns are changing and in what ways. Combining science with traditional teachings may hold the key to understanding how to adapt to these changes.

EAGLE FEATHERS

Elijah Harper, an Oji-Cree from northern Manitoba, became the first aboriginal member of the provincial Legislative Assembly in the 1980s. In 1990 he refused to give his consent for an agreement between Canada and the province of Quebec. He refused because the First Nations had not been consulted in the talks. His action delayed the accord long enough that it did not pass. In photographs taken in the legislature, he is shown holding an eagle feather.

MAKING A DIFFERENCE

In 1971, the Alaska Native Claims Settlement Act formed 12 Alaskan Native corporations and about

Melting ice in the Arctic is threatening some Native communities.

The mostly Native community of Cambridge Bay, Nunavut

200 village corporations. This act returned 44 million acres (17.8 million ha) to the Alaskan Nations. It also gave nearly $1 billion to the Nations. The creation of Canada's Nunavut territory in 1999 has given the Canadian Inuit a new home. Calls to cease polluting are another way people are working together to save the Arctic and Subarctic environments.

HOPE FOR THE FUTURE

Schools are getting help from elders to try to restore traditional teachings. Modern authors from the Cree,

Inuit, and other Nations are writing books and making films or artwork based on traditional stories and songs. Many are writing children's books that appeal to children of all cultures. Michael Kusugak's *A Promise Is a Promise* retells the story of Qallupilluit. Tomson Highway's *Caribou Song* tells of two Cree brothers who go hunting. These are only two examples. Children are also telling these stories in schools again. All these efforts are keeping the traditional stories of the Arctic and Subarctic Nations alive.

PERSPECTIVES
STORIES IN SCHOOLS

Many schools are helping preserve and share northern Nations' languages and cultures. For example, officials from an Ahtahkakoop Cree Nation school in Saskatchewan invited elders to their school. The elders shared stories in English and then in Cree, using oral traditions and teachings. Students took the opportunity to ask the elders questions about their culture.

STORY
SUMMARIES

Sedna, the Sea Mother (Inuit)

In one Inuit story, a woman falls into the sea. She sinks to the bottom of the sea to become a sea spirit. Her fingers become fish and ocean animals.

The Hero Kiviuq (Inuit)

An immortal hero named Kiviuq has many adventures. In one he follows a sandpiper. At first he sees only dark water. But he keeps following the sandpiper, and eventually he finds land.

The Game Mother (Tagish)

In one story from the Yukon, Game Mother teaches animals, such as moose, caribou, bears, and wolves, how to eat and behave. Then she creates a swing or hammock for them, where they all sing together before they leave to find their new homes throughout the land.

STOP AND
THINK

Tell the Tale

Chapters Three and Four discuss the lifestyle of the Inuit in the far north. Imagine you are taking a trip to Alaska or northern Canada. Write 200 words about the environment you encounter. How can you avoid harming the ecosystem?

Why Do I Care?

Chapters Four and Five discuss how climate change is altering the landscape in the Arctic and Subarctic regions. These changes are most visible in the far north, but they are happening around the globe. How might climate change affect you in the future?

You Are There

This book discusses many places in northern North America. Imagine you live in Alaska or northern Canada, and you are experiencing several weeks of night due to Earth's tilt. How would this affect your daily life?

Another View

This book talks about oral traditions in the Arctic and Subarctic. As you know, every source is different. Ask an adult to help you find a reliable source about this topic. Write a short essay comparing and contrasting the other source's point of view with that of this book's author. What is the point of view of each author? How are they similar and why? How are they different and why?

GLOSSARY

artifacts
human-made objects from long ago

climate
weather conditions over a long period of time

evergreen
trees that have leaves that stay green throughout the year

migrate
to move from one place to another, often due to the changing seasons

nomadic
moving from place to place

parka
a heavy winter coat that can be worn by men or women

shaman
an Inuit spiritual person who may be a healer or lead religious ceremonies

tundra
a type of landscape that is cold and treeless due to low temperatures and short growing seasons

LEARN MORE

Books

Gagne, Tammy. *Polar Bears Matter*. Minneapolis, MN: Abdo Publishing, 2016.

Lajiness, Katie. *Inuit*. Minneapolis, MN: Abdo Publishing, 2017.

Ollhoff, Jim. *Climate Change: Water and Ice*. Minneapolis, MN: Abdo Publishing, 2011.

Websites

To learn more about Native American Oral Histories, visit **abdobooklinks.com**. These links are routinely monitored and updated to provide the most current information available.

Visit **abdocorelibrary.com** for free additional tools for teachers and students.

INDEX

About the Author

Marie Powell lives on Treaty 4 land, in Regina, Saskatchewan. She has written more than 35 children's books and two young adult novels. Her favorite subjects to write about are science, history, and storytelling.